STRAIGHT TALK ON

Fear

STRAIGHT TALK ON

Fear

Overcoming Emotional Battles
with the
Power of God's Word!

JOYCE
MEYER

NEW YORK BOSTON NASHVILLE

Unless otherwise indicated, all Scripture quotations are taken from *The Amplified Bible* (AMP). *The Amplified Bible, Old Testament,* copyright © 1965, 1987 by Zondervan Corporation. *The Amplified Bible, New Testament,* copyright ©1954, 1958, 1987 by The Lockman Foundation. Used by permission.

Scripture quotations marked KJV are taken from the *King James Version* of the Bible.

Originally published as *Help Me I'm Afraid.*

Warner Books Edition
Copyright © 1998 by Joyce Meyer
Life In The Word, Inc.
P.O. Box 655
Fenton, Missouri 63026
All rights reserved.

Warner Faith

Time Warner Book Group
1271 Avenue of the Americas, New York, NY 10020
Visit our Web site at www.twbookmark.com.

Warner Faith® and the Warner Faith logo are trademarks of Time Warner Book Group Inc.

Printed in the United States of America

First Warner Faith Edition: October 2002
10 9 8 7 6 5 4 3

ISBN: 0-446-69198-4 (Special Sales Edition)

LCCN: 2002115537

CONTENTS

—————⟋∾⟍—————

INTRODUCTION

---❧---

One of the many benefits available to us in our spiritual inheritance as a believer in Jesus Christ is freedom from fear. But even if we are afraid, we know that we can go ahead and act, because God will be with us to protect us. He will help us, go before to fight the battle for us or deliver us, bringing us through victoriously as we obey Him.

If you feel you have missed out on some things in your life because of fear, you can learn how to handle or overcome fear and begin to experience the abundant life God has planned for you.

Part One

---◦∞◦---

FREEDOM FROM FEAR

I

CONFRONTING FEAR

. . . the Lord your God Who goes with you; He will not fail you or forsake you.

Deuteronomy 31:6

I

~⤬

CONFRONTING FEAR

$\mathcal{T}$he message of "fear not, for I, the Lord, am with you" is expressed in many different ways throughout the Bible. God does not want us to fear because fear prevents us from receiving and doing all He has planned for us. He loves and wants to bless us and has provided ways for us not to fear.

We can see in the following passage that we who believe in Jesus Christ do not need to fear the things that unbelievers—the people of "the world"—fear. God does not want us to fear those things.

> For the Lord spoke thus to me with His strong
> hand [upon me], and warned and instructed me
> not to walk in the way of this people, saying,

Do not call conspiracy [or hard, or holy] all that this people will call conspiracy [or hard, or holy]; neither be in fear of what they fear, nor [make others afraid and] in dread.

The Lord of hosts—regard Him as holy and honor His holy name [by regarding Him as your only hope of safety], and let Him be your fear and let Him be your dread [lest you offend Him by your fear of man and distrust of Him].

Isaiah 8:11–13

In His Word, God tells us that we can live victoriously, strong in Him and in the power of His might. And He has promised never to leave us or forsake us regardless of what happens.

No Fear!

Every one of us has experienced starting to step out in faith and, even at the thought of it, fear rising up in us. We need to realize that the source of fear is Satan. First John 4:18 KJV says:

There is no fear in love; but perfect love casteth
out fear; because fear hath torment. He that
feareth is not made perfect in love.

Satan sends fear to try to torment us into being so
doubtful and miserable, we will be prevented from doing
what God wants us to do and receiving all that God has
for us.

We can live without fear by building our faith on what
God has said in His Word. For example:

For God did not give us a spirit of timidity (of
cowardice, of craven and cringing and fawning
fear), but [He has given us a spirit] of power and
of love and of calm and well-balanced mind and
discipline and self-control.

2 Timothy 1:7

Be strong, courageous, and firm; fear not nor be
in terror before them, for it is the Lord your God
Who goes with you; He will not fail you or
forsake you.

Deuteronomy 31:6

Romans 10:17 KJV tells us, "So then faith cometh by hearing, and hearing by the word of God." We need to learn and confess aloud Scriptures like the ones above and the ones at the end of this book to drink them in like a glass of water when we are thirsty. When we open our mouth and confess what the Lord says to us and about us, God's Word will give us the power to overcome the fears that torment and prevent.

> And this is the confidence (the assurance, the privilege of boldness) which we have in Him: [we are sure] that if we ask anything (make any request) according to His will (in agreement with His own plan), He listens to and hears us.
>
> And if (since) we [positively] know that He listens to us in whatever we ask, we also know [with settled and absolute knowledge] that we have [granted us as our present possessions] the requests made of Him.
>
> 1 John 5:14,15

There is power in praying and confessing the Word of God, which is His revealed will. I am convinced that one of the most important things we can do in our prayer time is confessing the Word.

When we find ourselves trying to avoid confronting some issue in our life because of fear or dread or wondering or reasoning, what we should do is pray and ask God to do for us what He has promised in His Word—to go before us and pave the way for us. James teaches us that we have not because we ask not. (James 4:2.) Jesus tells us to ask, seek, and knock. (Matthew 7:7.)

When we are facing a job interview, for example, instead of being afraid that we will make a bad impression and fail to get the position, we need to ask the Lord to be with us, to go before us to prepare the way for us so that we can present ourselves in the very best light. Then we can trust that whatever happens, it will turn out for our good in accordance with God's perfect will and plan for us.

Do It Afraid!

Now [in Haran] the Lord said to Abram, Go for yourself [for your own advantage] away from your

country, from your relatives and your father's
house, to the land that I will show you.

Genesis 12:1

How would you feel if God told you to leave your
home, your family, and everything that is familiar and
comfortable to you and head out to who knows where?
Full of fear?

That is precisely the challenge Abram faced in this
passage—and it frightened him. That's why God kept saying to him again and again, "Fear not."

That is the same message He gave to Joshua when He
called him to lead the Children of Israel to take the land
He had promised to give them as their inheritance.
(Joshua 1:6,7,9)

Anyone who is going to do anything for God is going
to have to hear the Lord say on a regular basis, "Fear not."

Elisabeth Elliot, whose husband was killed along with
four other missionaries in Ecuador, tells that her life was
controlled completely by fear. Every time she started to
step out, fear stopped her. A friend told her something that
set her free. She said, "Why don't you do it afraid?" Elisabeth Elliot and Rachel Saint, sister of one of the murdered

missionaries, went on to evangelize the Indian tribes, including the people who had killed their husband and brother.

Many times we think we should wait to do something until we are not afraid. If we do that, we will probably accomplish very little for God, others, or even for ourselves. Both Abram and Joshua had to step out in faith and obedience to God and do what He had commanded them to do—afraid.

The Lord reminded me of the story about "Why don't you do it afraid?" then began showing me some things about fear.

"Fear Not" Means "Don't Run!"

. . . .Fear not; stand still (firm, confident, undismayed) and see the salvation of the Lord which He will work for you today. . . .

Exodus 14:13

What I perceived God was saying to me was that the phrase "Fear not" simply means "Don't run." Then the solution to fear is also simple. When we are faced with fear, rather than bowing our knee to it, we must stand firm against it and do what we fear anyway.

That is precisely what God tells us to do in His Word. Even if our knees are shaking, our mouth is dry and we feel as though we are about to fall down, we need to keep saying: "Lord, strengthen me. This is what You have told me to do, and with Your help I am going to do it, because it is Your revealed will for me. I am determined that my life is not going to be ruled by fear but by Your Word."

Confront Fear with God's Word

Fear cannot be by wished away or hoped away, it must be confronted and dealt with through God's Word.

There are times when people are miraculously delivered from fear through prayer. There is no doubt of that, because we serve a miracle-working God. I have prayed for people to be delivered from fear, and they have come back to me later and said, "After you prayed for me, I never had a problem with fear again." But the majority of the time, we confront and overcome our fears by meditating and speaking God's Word ourselves and resisting fear in the power of the Spirit.

In my own case, I had major problems as a result of the abuse I had suffered in my early years. There were many things in my life from which I needed deliverance. But with one minor exception, God delivered me from all of them as a result of my applying His Word. God doesn't always deliver us "from" things; often He walks us "through" them.

Fear Is Falsehood

> . . . the devil. . . . was a murderer from the
> beginning and does not stand in the truth,
> because there is no truth in him. When he
> speaks a falsehood, he speaks what is natural to
> him, for he is a liar [himself] and the father of lies
> and of all that is false.
>
> John 8:44

The Bible does not tell us "Tremble not" or "Sweat not" or "Shake not," it says, "Fear not."

There is a difference.

In this context, to fear is to take flight or to run from. Elisabeth Elliot's friend was suggesting that she start doing what she was afraid of instead of running from it.

It is said that the letters in the word "F-E-A-R" actually stand for "False Evidence Appearing Real."

Jesus said that the devil is a liar and the father of all lies. The truth is not in him. He tries to use falsehood to deceive God's people into fear so they will not be bold enough to be obedient to the Lord and reap the blessings He has in store for them.

Most of the time the fear of something is worse than the thing itself. Usually, if we will be courageous and determined enough to do whatever it is we fear, we will discover it is not nearly as bad as we thought it would be.

Throughout the Word of God we find the Lord saying to His people again and again, "Fear not." I believe the reason He did that was to encourage them so they would not allow Satan to rob them of their blessing.

In the same way, because He knows we are fearful, the Lord continues to exhort and encourage us to press through what lies before us to do what He is telling us to do. Why? Because He knows that great blessings await us on the other side.

We see an example of this in Abram.

Courage and Obedience Produce Great Rewards

After these things, the word of the Lord came to Abram in a vision, saying, Fear not, Abram, I am your Shield, your abundant compensation, and your reward shall be exceedingly great.

Genesis 15:1

As we saw before, in Genesis 12:1 God gave Abram a tall order. In so many words He said, "Pack up and leave everyone you know and everything you are comfortable with and go to a place I will show you."

If Abram had bowed his knee to fear, the rest of the story would never have come to pass. He would never have experienced God as his Shield, his great compensation, and he would never have received his exceedingly great reward.

In the same way, if Joshua had not overcome his fear and been obedient to God's command to lead His people into the Promised Land, neither he nor they would ever have enjoyed all that God had planned and prepared for them.

There is power in God's Word to equip us to stop bowing our knee in fear to the devil's desires. We can do what God wants us to do, even if we have to do it afraid.

2

PRAY ABOUT EVERYTHING AND FEAR NOTHING!

. . . The earnest (heartfelt, continued) prayer of a righteous man makes tremendous power available [dynamic in its working].

James 5:16

2

~⌒~

PRAY ABOUT EVERYTHING
AND FEAR NOTHING!

Some time ago the Lord spoke these words to me: "Pray about everything and fear nothing." He said this to me when I had a vague feeling of fear that a new hairdresser I was going to would not do a good job.

The Holy Spirit spoke to me: "Don't fear it, pray about it. Pray that the Lord will anoint this woman so she is able to do for you what needs to be done."

Then over the next couple of weeks He continued showing me different things about prayer versus fear. Many of them dealt with little areas in which fear would try to creep into my life and cause me problems. He showed me that in every case, no matter how great or important or how small or insignificant, the solution was to pray.

Fear not, [there is nothing to fear], for I am with you; do not look around you in terror and be dismayed, for I am your God. I will strengthen and harden you to difficulties, yes, I will help you; yes, I will hold you up and retain you with My [victorious] right hand of rightness and justice. . . .

For I the Lord your God hold your right hand; I am the Lord, Who says to you, Fear not; I will help you!

Isaiah 41:10,13

In this passage, the Lord tells His people not to look around them in terror or be dismayed, for He is their God.

Sometimes we become afraid just by staring at our circumstances. That is always a mistake. The more we focus our eyes and our mouths on the problem, the more fearful we become. Instead, we are to keep our eyes and our mouths focused on God. He is able to handle anything that we may ever have to face in this life.

God has promised to strengthen us, to harden us to difficulties, to hold us up and retain us with His victorious right hand. He also commands us not to be afraid. But remember, He is not commanding us never to feel fear, but rather not to let it control us.

The Lord is saying to you and me personally, "Fear not, I will help you." But we never experience the help of God until we place everything on the line, until we are obedient enough to step out in faith.

Do you know when I experience the anointing of God to preach? When I have walked up on the platform and begun to speak—not before, but *when* I have stepped out.

God is saying to us today, "Stop letting fear rule your life. Begin to do what I am telling you to do, because what I am telling you is for your benefit. I know the blessings that are on the other side, and so does the devil. That's why he is coming against you with fear and why I keep telling you to fear not."

Fear Not, You Are Mine!

. . . thus says the Lord, He Who created you, O Jacob, and He Who formed you, O Israel: Fear not, for I have redeemed you [ransomed you by paying a price instead of leaving you captives]; I have called you by your name; you are Mine.

21

When you pass through the waters, I will be with you, and through the rivers, they will not overwhelm you. When you walk through the fire, you will not be burned or scorched, nor will the flame kindle upon you.

Isaiah 43:1,2

Here the Lord is telling us not to fear when we go through trials of different kinds. That means we will experience victory in our lives, but only as we go through. If we are going to go through, then we must not run away anymore.

The Lord has promised to be with us and keep us safe when we go through the water, which will not overwhelm us, and through the fire, which will not burn us or scorch us.

Do you remember the story of the three Hebrew children named Shadrach, Meshach, and Abednego? They were thrown into a fiery furnace but came out of it not only unharmed but not even smelling like smoke! (Daniel 3:1–30.)

There are major fears—like being thrown into a trial similar to a fiery furnace—and there are also minor fears—like being afraid our hair won't look right!

We may be afraid of something major like cancer or a heart attack or the death of a loved one, or we may be afraid of something minor such as a picnic being rained out or not being able to find a parking place.

But whatever its magnitude or cause, fear is the same and must be dealt with the same way. As we have seen, it must be confronted through prayer with God's Word. And when we pray, we must believe. Fear is our enemy and we should treat it as such.

Faith: the Antidote for Fear

If any of you is deficient in wisdom, let him ask of the giving God [Who gives] to everyone liberally and ungrudgingly, without reproaching or faultfinding, and it will be given him.

Only it must be in faith that he asks with no wavering (no hesitating, no doubting). For the one who wavers (hesitates, doubts) is like the billowing surge out at sea that is blown hither and thither and tossed by the wind.

For truly, let not such a person imagine that he will receive anything [he asks for] from the Lord.

James 1:5–7

Faith is the only antidote for fear.

If you or I drank some kind of poison, we would have to swallow an antidote or the poison would cause serious damage or even death. The same is true of the deadly toxin of fear. There must be an antidote for it, and the only antidote for fear is faith.

When fear comes knocking at our door, we must answer it with faith, because nothing else is effective against it. And prayer is the major vehicle that carries faith.

Faith must be carried to the problem and released in some way. It is possible to pray without faith (we do it all the time), but it is impossible to have real faith and *not* pray.

James tells us that when we find ourselves in need of something, we should pray and ask God for it in *simple, believing* prayer. Those two words are very important. The way we do that is by simply praying and having faith, believing that what we ask for from God we will receive in accordance with His divine will and plan.

So the key to overcoming fear is simple, faith-filled, *continual* prayer.

Pray at All Times!

Pray at all times (on every occasion, in every season) in the spirit, with all [manner of] prayer and entreaty. To that end keep alert and watch with strong purpose and perseverance, interceding in behalf of all the saints (God's consecrated people).

Ephesians 6:18

In Ephesians 6:10–17 the apostle Paul talks about the armor of God and how we are to use it and the weapon of the Word to engage in spiritual warfare. After each piece has been listed, in verse 18 Paul sums up his message by saying, "Pray at all times. . . . "

How often are we to pray?

At all times.

How are we to pray?

In the Spirit, with all different kinds of prayer.

In the next chapter we will examine the different types of prayer, but right now let's consider praying "at all times."

What does that mean? Does it mean that when we are out doing the grocery shopping and God puts it on our heart to pray we are to drop to our knees right there in the middle of the supermarket aisle?

I often kneel by my bed and pray. There are other times when I feel led by God to lie down, face to the floor, before Him and pray. We have to be careful not to confuse posture with prayer. We can also pray silently in the supermarket as we are walking down the aisles.

In the different seasons of life we are able to pray in different ways. A young mother with three or four little children, for example, is going to have to structure her prayer life differently from that of a grandmother whose family is all grown up and out of the house.

If we become too "religious" about prayer, thinking we must do it one way or the other because that is how someone else does it, we will bring condemnation on ourselves. The important thing about prayer is not the posture or the time or place but learning to pray in faith—at all times, unceasingly. Anytime the desire or need arises . . . PRAY!

Pray Without Ceasing

Be unceasing in prayer [praying perseveringly].

1 Thessalonians 5:17

The *King James Version* of this verse says, "Pray without ceasing."

I used to read those words and wonder, "Lord, how can I ever get to the place that I am able to pray without ceasing?" To me the phrase "without ceasing" meant nonstop, without ever quitting.

I couldn't see how that was possible.

Now I have a better understanding of what Paul was saying. He meant that prayer should be like breathing, something we do continually but often unconsciously, without even being totally aware of it.

You and I live by breathing. Our physical bodies require it. In the same way, our spiritual bodies are designed to be nurtured and sustained by prayer.

The problem is that because of religious thinking we have gotten the mistaken idea that if we don't keep up a certain schedule of prayer we are missing the mark. We have become too clock-oriented concerning prayer.

The Lord gave me this example to illustrate the way we are to pray. Just as we breathe all day long but never spend time counting our breaths, so we are to pray all day long without keeping track of our prayers.

I have never carried a clock around with me to remind me to breathe every so many seconds. I have never come home from work at night and written down in a manual how many times I breathed that day. I just breathe when I need to, continually and continuously, without giving it a great deal of thought.

That's the way we are to be about our prayers.

I don't know how many times I pray a day; I pray all day long. I start praying when I get up in the morning, and I pray until I go to sleep at night. I enjoy special set-apart times for prayer as well as praying all throughout the day.

Does all this mean I never do anything else? No, there are periods when I have to give myself to other things. But I think as we consider the different type of prayers, we will see that we can pray at all times in every season, on every occasion, in every place, and that God will hear those prayers—which are just as spiritual and powerful as any others we may pray.

Do you know why the devil wants to make us feel so bad about our prayer life? Because he knows if he can make us feel that we are not doing it right, then we will do it out of obligation, but we won't be releasing any faith when we do it; therefore it won't do us any good.

Principles of Prayer

Now Peter and John were going up to the temple
at the hour of prayer. . . .

Acts 3:1

Many people feel vaguely guilty about their prayer life. There is no need because each person should have his or her own individual prayer life, and it doesn't have to be just like that of anyone else.

Yes, there are definite principles of prayer that need to be followed. It is good, for example, to discipline ourselves to have a certain time and place for prayer.

Even in the New Testament, as we see here in the book of Acts, the early disciples set aside certain hours of the day when they would go to a designated place to pray. That is good self-discipline, and there is nothing wrong with it. But that should be the start of prayer and not the finish.

The point is that we should discipline ourselves to establish a prayer schedule that is individually suited to us and then stick to it until it becomes such a part of our lifestyle that we do it without even thinking.

There was a time when I had to discipline myself to brush my teeth. But I have done that so long now I don't even think about it any more, I just do it. I brush my teeth before I go to bed at night, when I get up in the morning, and after every meal. Teeth brushing is just a normal part of my everyday life.

The same holds true when we start our walk with the Lord. At first we may have to discipline ourselves in some areas because we are so undisciplined in those areas. But after a while they should become such a normal part of our lives that we do them without even thinking.

I believe if we will allow Him to do so, the Holy Spirit will lead us into prayer without ceasing so it becomes like breathing. When that happens we can be continually offering up prayers.

We can get up every day saying, "Good morning, Lord, I love You." We can go to the breakfast table saying, "Father, You are so good to me." We can drive to work saying, "Thank You, God, for all the good things You are going to do for me today."

Throughout the day and evening we can continue to communicate with the Lord, praising and worshiping Him, thanking Him for His presence with us and asking His help in all our problems. Then just before we go to sleep at night, we can offer up a final prayer of gratitude for the blessings of the day and a request for a peaceful and refreshing night's sleep.

Now the devil may try to tell us that is not praying because we are not in the right posture or not praying in formal "church language." That is the time to kick the devil in the teeth! Because prayer is not of the body, or even of the mouth; it is of the spirit, the mind and the heart.

And where there is prayer, there is power!

Prayer Is Power!

. . . The earnest (heartfelt, continued) prayer of a
righteous man makes tremendous power
available [dynamic in its working].

James 5:16

Simple, believing prayer is powerful! In fact, there is
nothing more powerful than heartfelt, continued prayer!

The reason the devil torments us about our prayer life
and tries to prevent us from being faithful to it is because
he wants us in a weakened condition. He knows it is continual, believing prayer that destroys his works and ushers
in the will of God on this earth.

Anytime you and I begin to feel guilty about our
prayer life, we begin to lose the ability to release our faith
through it.

In order to accomplish what God has called us to do
in this life, we need to be assured He does hear our prayers
and does respond to them. That is what makes them so
powerful and so effective.

That's why we need to stop fearing and start continually praying—in faith—all kinds of prayers!

3

TYPES OF PRAYER

*First of all, then, I admonish and urge that
petitions, prayers, intercessions, and thanksgivings
be offered on behalf of all men.*

1 Timothy 2:1

3

~

TYPES OF PRAYER

First of all, then, I admonish and urge that
petitions, prayers, intercessions, and thanks-
givings be offered on behalf of all men,

For kings and all who are in positions of
authority or high responsibility, that
[outwardly] we may pass a quiet and undis-
turbed life [and inwardly] a peaceable one in
all godliness and reverence and seriousness in
every way.

For such [praying] is good and right, and [it is]
pleasing and acceptable to God our Savior.

1 Timothy 2:1–3

$\mathcal{A}$s we see here in this passage, we are to pray all types of
prayers for ourselves and for others.

Let's look at some of the different types of prayers that we are to pray as we engage in continual, heartfelt prayer.

Prayer of Commitment

Commit your way to the Lord [roll and repose each care of your load on Him]; trust (lean on, rely on, and be confident) also in Him and He will bring it to pass.

Psalm 37:5

First there is the prayer of commitment in which we commit ourselves and our lives to the Lord. We do that when we cast our load of care upon Him as we are told to do in 1 Peter 5:7: "Cast . . . the whole of your care [all your anxieties, all your worries, all your concerns, once and for all] on Him, for He cares for you affectionately and cares about you watchfully."

When we are faced with fears and problems that threaten to overwhelm and destroy us, we need to pray: "Lord, I am not going to carry this load of care around with me and allow it to torment me and prevent me from serving You.

"I am praying right now, Father, that You will strengthen me and enable me to do what You have called me to do even if I have to do it afraid.

"I cast this situation on You, God. Whatever evil, wicked, perverted thing the devil is trying to tell me is going to happen, that is Your problem, and not mine, because I am going to do what You have told me to do and leave the rest to You."

The minute fear arises, if you and I will pray, sooner or later we will see it overcome by the power of God.

The problem is that many times it is not the major fears that cause us the most trouble. Like the little foxes that spoil the vineyards (Song of Solomon 2:15), often it is all those little pestering fears that assail us day and night that drain the life out of us and steal our joy.

That's why, at the very first sign of fear, no matter how minor it may be, we need to confront it and pray, "Lord, I will not live in fear. Instead, I commit my way unto You and ask You to overcome this thing that is trying to torment and prevent me from living the abundant life You desire for me and fulfilling Your good and perfect will and plan for me."

If we will do that in heartfelt, earnest prayer, the Lord will honor our request and commitment and will do His part to keep us free.

Prayer of Consecration or Dedication

I appeal to you therefore, brethren, and beg of you in view of [all] the mercies of God, to make a decisive dedication of your bodies [presenting all your members and faculties] as a living sacrifice, holy (devoted, consecrated) and well pleasing to God, which is your reasonable (rational, intelligent) service and spiritual worship.

Romans 12:1

When we give something to God in prayer, that is a prayer of consecration or dedication. We say in essence, "Here, Lord, I give You my money, my time, my mind"—whatever it may be.

The apostle Paul tells us here in this passage that we are to give, dedicate, consecrate to the Lord our bodies, all our members and faculties, for His use, which is our reasonable service and worship.

We also pray the prayer of consecration or dedication when we dedicate our children to God, promising to " . . . bring them up in the nurture and admonition of the Lord" (Ephesians 6:4 KJV).

Just as we dedicate and consecrate our lives, our money and possessions, our minds and bodies, ourselves and our children to God, so we also ought to dedicate and consecrate our mouths—which leads us to the next type of prayer.

Prayer of Praise and Worship

Through Him, therefore, let us constantly and at
all times offer up to God a sacrifice of praise,
which is the fruit of lips that thankfully acknowledge and confess and glorify His name.

Hebrews 13:15

I think we all understand praise and worship.

Praise is really recounting the goodness of God. It is telling the story of all the good things He has done for us.

Worship is simply adoring God. It is acknowledging His "worth-ship." It is recognizing Him for Who He is and what He is.

That's why the writer of the book of Hebrews tells us that we should be praising and worshiping God constantly and at all times.

As we have seen, the prayer of praise and worship should be like breathing, in and out, day and night, moment by moment.

We are to be thankful to God always, continually acknowledging, confessing, and glorifying His name in prayerful praise and worship.

Prayer of Thanksgiving

Thank [God] in everything [no matter what the circumstances may be, be thankful and give thanks], for this is the will of God for you [who are] in Christ Jesus [the Revealer and mediator of that will].

1 Thessalonians 5:18

Immediately after telling us in 1 Thessalonians 5:17 to pray without ceasing, the apostle Paul directs us in verse

18 to give thanks to God in everything, no matter what our circumstances may be, stating that this is the will of God for us.

Just as prayer is to be a lifestyle for us, so thanksgiving is to be a lifestyle for us.

Giving thanks to God should not be something we do once a day as we sit down somewhere and try to think of all the good things He has done for us and merely say, "Thanks, Lord."

That is religion, something we do simply because we think God requires it.

True thanksgiving flows continually out of a heart that is full of gratitude and praise to God for Who He is as much as for what He does. It is not something that is done to meet a requirement, win favor, gain a victory, or qualify for a blessing.

The type of thanksgiving that God the Father desires is that which is provoked by the presence of His Holy Spirit within us Who moves upon us to express to the Lord verbally what we are feeling and experiencing spiritually.

True thanksgiving is the kind expressed by the psalmist when he wrote: "O give thanks to the Lord of lords, for His mercy and loving-kindness endure forever—" (Psalm 136:3)!

Prayer in the Spirit

> But you, beloved, build yourselves up [founded] on your most holy faith [make progress, rise like an edifice higher and higher], praying in the Holy Spirit.
>
> Jude 20

We have already seen in Ephesians 6:18 that we are not only to pray at all times with all manner of prayers, but as we are told here by Jude, our prayers are to be "in the Holy Spirit."

It is the Holy Spirit of God within us Who provokes us and leads us to pray. Rather than delaying, we need to learn to yield to the leading of the Spirit as soon as we sense it. That is part of learning to pray all manner of prayers at all times, wherever we may be, and whatever we may be doing.

Our motto should be that of the old spiritual song, "Every time I feel the Spirit moving in my heart, I will pray."

If we know we can pray anytime and anywhere, we won't feel we have to wait until just the right moment or place to pray.

Prayer of Agreement

Again I tell you, if two of you on earth agree
(harmonize together, make a symphony together)
about whatever [anything and everything] they
may ask, it will come to pass and be done for
them by My Father in heaven.

For wherever two or three are gathered
(drawn together as My followers) in (into) My
name, there I AM in the midst of them.

Matthew 18:19,20

There is power in agreement.

The Bible tells us that if the Lord is with them one can chase a thousand, and two can put ten thousand to flight. (Deuteronomy 32:30). But that power is available only to those who are in agreement with each other—and with God.

Obviously we cannot argue and fight with one another all the time and then agree in prayer on some need and expect that "prayer of agreement" to be effective, as we are told in 1 Peter 3:7: "In the same way you married men should live considerately with [your wives], with an intelligent recognition [of the marriage relation], honoring the woman as [physically] the weaker, but [realizing that you] are joint heirs of the grace (God's unmerited favor) of life, in order that your prayers may not be hindered and cut off. [Otherwise you cannot pray effectively.]"

In the same way, we cannot gossip and complain about the preacher all week long and then go to him for prayer about some serious personal problem and expect him to pray the prayer of agreement with us.

Why not? Because we are already *out* of agreement—with each other and with God.

Do you know why God honors the prayer of agreement? Because He knows what a challenge it is to walk and live in agreement. He respects anyone who will do that.

If you and I will come into agreement with each other and with God, then there will be an added force behind our prayers to make them much more powerful and effective.

United or Corporate Prayer

All of these with their minds in full agreement
devoted themselves steadfastly to prayer. . . .

Acts 1:14

There is great power in united or corporate prayer,
which as we see here in this verse is a form of prayer in
agreement.

Throughout the book of Acts we read that the people
of God came together "with one accord." (Acts 2:1,46;
4:24; 5:12; 15:25 kjv.)

Then in Philippians 2:2 we are told by the apostle
Paul, "Fill up and complete my joy by living in harmony
and being of the same mind and one in purpose, having
the same love, being in full accord and of one harmonious
mind and intention."

If we will heed these words and come into harmony
and agreement with each other and with God, we will
experience the same kind of powerful results the first-
century disciples enjoyed in the book of Acts.

Prayer of Intercession

I exhort therefore, that, first of all, supplications, prayers, intercessions, and giving of thanks, be made for all men.

1 Timothy 2:1 KJV

To intercede for someone is to "stand in the gap" for him, to plead his case before the throne of God.

In Romans 8:26,27 KJV we are told by the apostle Paul that the Holy Spirit makes intercession for us according to the will of the Lord.

In Hebrews 7:25 we read that Jesus " . . . is always living to make petition to God and intercede with Him and intervene . . . " for us.

Finally, Paul exhorts us here in 1 Timothy 2:1 KJV to make intercession "for all men," meaning that we are to pray for all people everywhere.

Intercession is one of the most important ways we carry on the ministry of Jesus Christ which He began in this earth.

Prayer of Silence

... the Lord is in His holy temple; let all the
earth hush and keep silence before Him.

Habakkuk 2:20

I also call this kind of prayer "waiting on the Lord."

David knew all about waiting on the Lord as we see in
Psalm 27:4 in which he wrote: "One thing have I asked of
the Lord, that will I seek, inquire for, and [insistently]
require: that I may dwell in the house of the Lord [in His
presence] all the days of my life, to behold and gaze upon
the beauty [the sweet attractiveness and the delightful
loveliness] of the Lord and to meditate, consider, and
inquire in His temple."

It is very important to learn to wait on the Lord
because most people don't understand that waiting is a
vital part of prayer.

Prayer is not just doing, it is also an attitude of waiting. Prayer is not talking to God all the time—it is also listening to Him.

Prayer of Petition

Do not fret or have any anxiety about anything,
but in every circumstance and in everything, by
prayer and petition (definite requests), with
thanksgiving, continue to make your wants
known to God.

Philippians 4:6

Petition is simply making requests, asking God to meet needs.

I always say that the greatest prayer anyone can pray is what I call the "help-me" prayer: "Help me, God, help me, help me! Oh, God, help me!"

I pray that prayer a lot.

Sometimes I get up in the middle of the night to go to the bathroom, and there is not a think wrong with me; yet I will find myself praying, "Oh God, help me, help me!"

I believe I am led by the Holy Spirit to pray that way.

"Help me, God!" is a powerful prayer. If you and I can do nothing else, we can always pray that way.

Another important prayer of petition is simply: "God I need You."

You and I will see major changes take place in our lives if we will stop trying to do everything ourselves.

Proverbs 3:5–7 tells us: "Lean on, trust in, and be confident in the Lord with all your heart and mind and do not rely on your own insight and understanding. In all your ways know, recognize, and acknowledge Him, and He will direct and make straight and plain your paths. Be not wise in your own eyes; reverently fear and worship the Lord and turn [entirely] away from evil."

Don't wait until after you have already fallen apart and proven that you can't handle things on your own before you run to God for help. Know ahead of time that you can't before you even try. Be totally dependent on God.

Learn to pray: "Lord, I can't do this, but You can. Do this through me. I am leaning on, trusting in, and being confident in You with all my heart and mind. Help me, Lord, because I need You."

Just that little prayer of petition is enough to see you through the worst situations of life.

Acknowledging God takes only a few minutes but it can help us to avoid many failures in our everyday life—especially when we realize that without God we can do nothing.

When we have said, "Lord, I am depending on You, please help me," we have prayed the prayer of petition—and it is powerful. Prayers of petition are also requests to have wants, needs or desires met. We should be comfortable talking to the Lord about anything that concerns us. Remember, He loves us very much and is concerned about anything that concerns us.

Put First Things First!

Now while they were on their way, it occurred that Jesus entered a certain village, and a woman named Martha received and welcomed Him into her house.

And she had a sister named Mary, who seated herself at the Lord's feet and was listening to His teaching.

But Martha [overly occupied and too busy] was distracted with much serving; and she came up to Him and said, Lord, is it nothing to You that my sister has left me to serve alone? Tell her then to help me [to lend a hand and do her part along with me]!

But the Lord replied to her by saying,
Martha, Martha you are anxious and troubled
about many things;

There is need of only one or but a few things.
Mary has chosen the good portion [that which is
to her advantage], which shall not be taken away
from her.

Luke 10:38–42

By now you may have begun to realize that you may have a better prayer life than you thought. You have seen that although it is good to have a set time and a specific place to pray to the Lord, especially at the beginning of each day, actually there is great power in being in prayer all the time.

The way to develop a powerful, effective prayer life is by simply spending time in the presence of the Lord. As followers of Christ, that is what our lifestyle should be centered around.

If you and I will just sit in the Lord's presence for a period of time before we start our day, and then remain conscious of that presence throughout the rest of the day, we will see marvelous results in our everyday life.

If you think you don't have time, remember this rule: "The busier I get, the more time I need to spend with God." After all, the more I have to do, the more I need His help.

If, like Martha, you are too busy to spend time with the Lord, then you are just plain too busy. You need to be more like Mary and learn to let some lesser things go for a while so you can sit at the feet of the Lord and learn from Him.

If you will do that, you will receive from Him the very keys to the Kingdom!

4

❧

KEYS TO THE KINGDOM

I will give you the keys of the kingdom of heaven. . . .

Matthew 16:19

4

∿

KEYS TO THE KINGDOM

*Now when Jesus went into the region of Caesarea
Philippi, He asked His disciples, Who do people
say that the Son of Man is?*

*And they answered, Some say John the Baptist;
others say Elijah; and others Jeremiah or one of the
prophets.*

*He said to them, But who do you [yourselves]
say that I am?*

*Simon Peter replied, You are the Christ, the Son
of the living God.*

Matthew 16:13–16

When Peter made that statement about Jesus being the
Christ, the Son of the Living God, he was releasing with
his mouth the faith that was in his heart.

We must understand that we establish the faith that is in our heart by the words we speak from our mouth, as we read in Romans 10:10: "For with the heart a person believes (adheres to, trusts in, and relies on Christ) and so is justified (declared righteous, acceptable to God), and with the mouth he confesses (declares openly and speaks out freely his faith) and confirms [his] salvation."

That is why prayer is so important. Because we establish the things we believe inwardly when we start talking about them outwardly.

That is also why confessing Scripture in prayer is so important. When we do that, we are establishing things in the spiritual realm by the words we are speaking in the physical realm. And eventually what is established spiritually will be manifested physically.

You and I should be constantly confessing the Word of God. We should be saying things like:

"Father, I believe in You. I believe You love me so much You sent Your Son Jesus to die for me on the cross.

"I believe you have filled me with Your Holy Spirit. I believe You have a good plan for my life, and You are empowering me to fulfill it.

"I believe Your anointing is upon me so I can lay hands on the sick and they will recover, and cast out devils and they will flee.

"I believe that in accordance with Your Word, everything I put my hand to prospers and succeeds."

On and on we should go, believing in our heart and confessing with our mouth what God has said about us in His Word.

And one thing He has said about is that He has not given us a spirit of fear but of power and of love and of a sound mind. Therefore, we should be confessing continually, "I will not fear!"

Faith Shall Prevail

Then Jesus answered him, Blessed (happy, fortunate, and to be envied) are you, Simon Bar-Jonah. For flesh and blood [men] have not revealed this to you, but My Father Who is in heaven.

And I tell you, you are Peter [Greek, *Petros*—a large piece of rock], and on this rock [Greek, *petra*—a huge rock like Gibraltar] I will

build My church, and the gates of Hades (the
powers of the infernal region) shall not over-
power it [or be strong to its detriment or hold out
against it].

Matthew 16:17,18

What rock is Jesus talking about in this passage? He
is talking about the rock of faith. He is telling Simon
Peter that on the faith he has just displayed He will
build His Church, and (as the *King James Version* puts
it) " . . . the gates of hell shall not prevail against it"
(v. 18).

That means that the gates of hell shall not prevail
against the person who walks in faith.

Fear comes from hell. That's why John tells us that
" . . . fear hath torment . . . " (1 John 4:18 KJV). But when
fear is confronted by faith, hell cannot prevail against it.

The Keys to the Kingdom

I will give you the keys of the kingdom of heaven;
and whatever you bind (declare to be improper
and unlawful) on earth must be what is already

bound in heaven; and whatever you loose
(declare lawful) on earth must be what is already
loosed in heaven.

Matthew 16:19

What Jesus was saying here is, "Whatever is taking place in heaven, I am giving you the power and authority to bring to pass in the earth."

This is the fulfillment of the prayer to the Father that Jesus had taught the disciples to pray in Matthew 6:10: "Your kingdom come, Your will be done on earth as it is in heaven."

Later on in Matthew 18:18 Jesus gave this same power to bind and loose to all the disciples when He said to them: "Truly I tell you, whatever you forbid and declare to be improper and unlawful on earth must be what is already forbidden in heaven, and whatever you permit and declare proper and lawful on earth must be what is already permitted in heaven."

What Jesus was telling them was that He was conferring upon them the power and authority to use the keys He was giving them to bring to pass on earth the will of God that prevails in heaven.

I believe the keys He gave to Peter and the other disciples—and to us—may be references to the different types of prayer we have been studying.

Earnest Prayer Is Effectual

. . . The effectual fervent prayer of a righteous
man availeth much.

Elias was a man subject to like passions as
we are, and he prayed earnestly that it might not
rain: and it rained not on the earth by the space
of three years and six months.

And he prayed again, and the heaven gave
rain, and the earth brought forth her fruit.

James 5:16–18 KJV

In any organization, who has the power and authority? Isn't it the person who controls the keys? What do keys do? They lock and unlock. That is what binding and loosing mean—locking and unlocking.

When you and I intercede for someone, for example, we unlock a blessing on that person's life. We unlock the door of hell that is holding him or her in bondage.

In the same way, when we offer a prayer of thanksgiving to God, we are unlocking a blessing in our own life.

So you and I have been given the keys to the Kingdom of God. With those prayer keys we have the authority and the power to bring to pass the will of God on earth as it is in heaven.

What a privilege!

No wonder the devil wants to deceive us into thinking that our prayer life is ineffectual—so we will give up and quit rather than continuing to use the key ring of prayers to overcome his kingdom of darkness.

Don't let the devil belittle you concerning your prayer life. Begin to acknowledge God, calling upon Him in prayer—all kinds of prayer—trusting that your earnest, heartfelt prayers *are* effectual because your faith is in Him not in your own ability to live holy or pray eloquently.

Prayer as Requisition

Do not fret or have any anxiety about anything,
but in every circumstance and in everything, by
prayer and petition (definite requests), with

thanksgiving, continue to make your wants
known to God.

Philippians 4:6

We looked at this passage when we talked about the
prayer of petition.

What is a petition? According to this verse it is a
definite request. Another word for a definite request is a
requisition.

What is a requisition? It is a demand or request made
on something to which a person is legally entitled but not
yet in possession of, as in the military when an officer requisitions equipment or supplies for his men. As a duly
commissioned agent of the United States Army, he is entitled to that material, but in order to receive it he has to
submit a definite request for it.

The Lord has shown me that when we pray, what we
are doing is requisitioning from Him what He has already
set aside to provide for us when the need arises.

Let me give you an example from everyday life. You
and I may have money in a bank. But in order for us to
benefit from that money we must requisition it by writing

a check, which is a request to the bank to issue to us or to the person we designate a certain sum of money for a certain purpose.

The same thing happens when managers come to my husband, who is the financial officer of our ministry, asking for money for their departments. Before he will release any funds to them, although that is what the money is set aside for, they must submit a written requisition for it stating the amount requested and the purpose for which it will be used.

That is what prayer is—a heavenly requisition we submit to God for what we need to carry on our daily life and ministry.

Ask in Jesus' Name

So for the present you are also in sorrow (in distress and depressed); but I will see you again and [then] your hearts will rejoice, and no one can take from you your joy (gladness, delight).

And when that time comes, you will ask nothing of Me [you will need to ask Me no questions]. I assure you, most solemnly I tell you, that My Father will grant you whatever you ask in My name [as presenting all that I AM].

John 16:22,23

The Bible teaches that God knows everything about us. (Psalm 139:1–6.) He knows what we have need of before we ask Him. (Matthew 6:8,32.) Yet He has commanded that we ask. (Matthew 7:7.)

You and I do not receive the things we need by wishing. To go around saying "I wish I had more money" or "I wish I could get rid of this headache" or "I wish I could live without fear" is not a heavenly requisition.

According to what we read in James 1:5–8 we have got to ask for what we need in faith, believing that we receive what we ask for, what we have requisitioned from God's storehouse of blessings.

Here in this passage from John 16, spoken by Jesus to His disciples just before He went to the cross, He makes it clear that when we pray we must not only believe but we must also ask in His name.

Now that does not mean just tacking the phrase "in Jesus' name" on the end of everything we say. If we are not careful we can become so religious that every sentence that comes our of our mouth ends with "hallelujah," "praise God," or "in Jesus' name." When that happens, those words soon lose their meaning.

That is not what Jesus was talking about. He was talking about using the authority of His name, as He has commanded us to do, in order to bring about the will of God on earth as it is in heaven. He was talking about submitting a requisition to God the Father over the signature of His Son for what we need to usher in His Kingdom.

In our ministry, our employees earn vacation time. It is legally theirs. But even though it rightfully belongs to them, they cannot receive a day of that vacation time unless they submit a requisition for it.

You and I have an inheritance laid up for us in heaven, bought and paid for by the shed blood of Jesus Christ. (Ephesians 1:11,12.) It is legally and rightfully ours. But the problem is that we have not been submitting enough requisitions.

If an employee of our ministry submits a requisition to Dave, our finance manager, and that person does not receive the authorization to take that earned vacation, he soon comes to Dave and asks, "Did you lose my requisition? When am I going to get what is rightfully mine?"

When you and I submit a requisition to God in the name of Jesus, and we do not receive what we have asked for in faith, then we have every right to go to the Lord and ask Him, "Father, You haven't forgotten about my requisition, have You?" That is not impudence, it is faith. It actually honors the Lord because it shows Him that we expect Him to keep His Word because He is faithful.

Use the Name of Jesus!

Up to this time you have not asked a [single] thing in My Name [as presenting all that I AM]; but now ask and keep on asking and you will receive, so that your joy (gladness, delight) may be full and complete.

John 16:24

Jesus commanded us to ask in His name that we might receive so that our joy might be full.

I am convinced that one of the main reasons for the lack of joy in the life of believers today is a lack of prayer.

And one reason for the lack of prayer is the fact that God's people are trying to do in the flesh what they should be praying about and asking God to do through them and for them.

Jesus told His disciples that after He was resurrected from the dead, things would be different. He told them they would have a new power and authority they had not enjoyed before His death and resurrection.

"When that time comes," He told them, "you won't have to ask Me anything, but you can go straight to the Father, and He will grant you whatever you ask—in My name."

What does it mean to ask in Jesus' name?

According to verse 24, to pray in the name of Jesus is to present to the Father all that Jesus is.

One of the main reasons we are so weak in prayer power is because we go to God trying to present to Him what we are. The problem with that is that if we have failed Him in any way, we think we have nothing to present to Him that will influence Him to act on our behalf.

The Bible says that in the sight of God all our righteousness is as filthy rags. (Isaiah 64:6 KJV.) So there is nothing that you and I can present to God except the blood of Jesus.

That's why I am so excited about my book titled *The Word, The Name, The Blood* (see the book list in the back). In it I discuss this very issue.

As you and I come before the throne of God's grace, covered with the blood of Jesus, asking in faith according to His Word and in the name of His Son Jesus Christ, we can know that we have the petitions that we ask of Him. Not because we are perfect or worthy of ourselves, or because God owes us anything, but because He loves us and wants to give us what we need to do the job He has called us to do.

There is power in the name of Jesus. At the very mention of it, every knee has to bow in heaven, on earth, and beneath the earth. (Philippians 2:10.) By the power of that name you and I are to lay hands on the sick and they will recover, cast out demons and they will flee, and do the same works that Jesus did and even greater works than these for the glory of God. (Mark 16:17,18; John 14:12.)

Jesus has purchased a glorious inheritance for us by the shedding of His blood. We are now joint-heirs with Him. (Romans 8:17 KJV.) Everything that He has earned by his sacrifice is in the heavenlies stored up for us. We have the keys to that storehouse, and the keys are prayer.

We do not have to live in fear and lack. Let's start using those keys and opening those doors so that heavenly blessings may be showered down upon us for the glory of God, so that His divine will may be done on earth as it is in heaven, and so that our joy may be made complete.

Conclusion

❧

$\mathcal{F}$ear is not from God. Fear is from Satan.

The only acceptable attitude (and confession) that a Christian can have toward fear is this: "It is not from God, and I will not put up with it or let it control my life! *I will confront fear,* for it is a spirit sent out from hell to torment me."

I often say that fear is the spirit Satan uses to try to keep God's people from coming under the leadership of the true Master, Jesus Christ.

I believe God works gently with us in areas to bring us out of bondage and into liberty. The Bible is full of instructions to "Fear not." As mentioned before, events in my own life have led me to understand that "Fear not" means "Do not run."

I encourage you to press on, and if need be "do it afraid." Don't run from fear; instead, confront it in prayer and faith.

Remember, God wants to deliver you from *all* your fear:

F - False

E - Evidence

A - Appearing

R - Real

Part Two

Part Two

—❧—

SCRIPTURES

SCRIPTURES
TO OVERCOME FEAR

—⟋∾⟍—

. . . Fear not; stand still (firm, confident,
undismayed) and see the salvation of the Lord
which He will work for you today. . . .

Exodus 14:13

Behold, the Lord your God has set the land
before you; go up and possess it, as the Lord, the
God of your fathers, has said to you. Fear not,
neither be dismayed.

Deuteronomy 1:21

Be strong, courageous, and firm; fear not nor be
in terror before them, for it is the Lord your God

Who goes with you; He will not fail you or
forsake you.

Deuteronomy 31:6

Have not I commanded you? Be strong, vigorous,
and very courageous. Be not afraid, neither be
dismayed, for the Lord your God is with you
wherever you go.

Joshua 1:9

Fear not [there is nothing to fear], for I am with
you; do not look around you in terror and be
dismayed, for I am your God. I will strengthen
and harden you to difficulties, yes, I will help
you; yes, I will hold you up and retain you with
My [victorious] right hand of rightness and
justice. . . .

For I the Lord your God hold your right
hand; I am the Lord, Who says to you, Fear not; I
will help you!

Isaiah 41:10,13

. . . thus says the Lord, He Who created you, O
Jacob, and He who formed You, O Israel: Fear
not, for I have redeemed you [ransomed you by
paying a price instead of leaving you captives]; I
have called you by your name; you are Mine.

When you pass through the waters, I will be
with you, and through the rivers, they will not
overwhelm you. When you walk through the fire,
you will not be burned or scorched, nor will the
flame kindle upon you.

Isaiah 43:1,2

For [the Spirit which] you have now received [is]
not a spirit of slavery to put you once more in
bondage to fear, but you have received the Spirit
of adoption [the Spirit producing sonship] in [the
bliss of] which we cry, Abba (Father)! Father!

Romans 8:15

And do not [for a moment] be frightened or
intimidated in anything by your opponents and
adversaries, for such [constancy and fearlessness]

will be a clear sign (proof and seal) to them of [their impending] destruction, but [a sure token and evidence] of your deliverance and salvation, and that from God.

Philippians 1:28

Do not fret or have any anxiety about anything, but in every circumstance and in everything, by prayer and petition (definite requests), with thanksgiving, continue to make your wants known to God.

And God's peace [shall be yours, that tranquil state of a soul assured of its salvation through Christ, and so fearing nothing from God and being content with its earthly lot of whatever sort that is, that peace] which transcends all understanding shall garrison and mount guard over your hearts and minds in Christ Jesus.

Philippians 4:6,7

For God did not give us a spirit of timidity (of cowardice, of craven and cringing and fawning fear), but [He has given us a spirit] of power and of love and of calm and well-balanced mind and discipline and self-control.

2 Timothy 1:7

Let your character or moral disposition be free from love of money [including greed, avarice, lust, and craving for earthly possessions] and be satisfied with your present [circumstances with with what you have]; for He [God] Himself has said, I will not in any way fail you nor give you up nor leave you without support. [I will] not, [I will] not, [I will] not in any degree leave you helpless nor forsake nor let [you] down (relax My hold on you)! [Assuredly not!]

So we take comfort and are encouraged and confidently and boldly say, The Lord is my Helper; I will not be seized with alarm [I will not fear or dread or be terrified]. What can man do to me?

Hebrews 13:5,6

There is no fear in love [dread does not exist], but full-grown (complete, perfect) love turns fear out of doors and expels every trace of terror! For fear brings with it the thought of punishment, and [so] he who is afraid has not reached the full maturity of love [is not yet grown into love's complete perfection].

1 John 4:18

Prayer to Combat Fear

—∾⌾∾—

Oh, God, deliver me from fear. Help me to be courageous and to have holy boldness.

Help me to "fear not" but to go in and possess all You desire for me to have.

Help me to know how much You love me, because perfect love (Your love for me) will cast out all fear. In Jesus' name, amen.

PRAYER FOR A
PERSONAL RELATIONSHIP
WITH THE LORD

If you have never invited Jesus, the Prince of Peace, to be your Lord and Savior, I invite you to do so now. Pray the following prayer, and if you are really sincere about it, you will experience a new life in Christ.

Father,

You loved the world so much, You gave Your only begotten Son to die for our sins so that whoever believes in Him will not perish, but have eternal life.

Your Word says we are saved by grace through faith as a gift from You. There is nothing we can do to earn salvation.

I believe and confess with my mouth that Jesus Christ is Your Son, the Savior of the world. I believe He died on the cross for me and bore all of my sins, paying the price for them. I believe in my heart that You raised Jesus from the dead.

I ask You to forgive my sins. I confess Jesus as my Lord. According to Your Word, I am saved and will spend eternity with You! Thank You, Father. I am so grateful! In Jesus' name, amen.

See John 3:16; Ephesians 2:8,9; Romans 10:9,10; 1 Corinthians 15:3,4; John 1:9; 4:14–16; 5:1,12,13.

About the Author

---◦∾◦---

Joyce Meyer has been teaching the Word of God since 1976 and in full-time ministry since 1980. She is the bestselling author of more than sixty inspirational books, including *In Pursuit of Peace, How to Hear from God, Knowing God Intimately*, and *Battlefield of the Mind*. She has also released thousands of teaching cassettes and a complete video library. Joyce's *Enjoying Everyday Life* radio and television programs are broadcast around the world, and she travels extensively conducting conferences. Joyce and her husband, Dave, are the parents of four grown children and make their home in St. Louis, Missouri.

To contact the author write:

Joyce Meyer Ministries
P. O. Box 655
Fenton, Missouri 63026
or call: (636) 349-0303
Internet Address: www.joycemeyer.org

Please include your testimony or help received from this book when you write. Your prayer requests are welcome.

To contact the author
in Canada, please write:
Joyce Meyer Ministries Canada, Inc.
Lambeth Box 1300
London, ON N6P 1T5
or call: (636) 349-0303

In Australia, please write:
Joyce Meyer Ministries—Australia
Locked Bag 77
Mansfield Delivery Centre
Queensland 4122
or call: 07 3349 1200

In England, please write:
Joyce Meyer Ministries
P. O. Box 1549
Windsor
SL4 1GT
or call: (0) 1753-831102

JOYCE MEYER TITLES

Healing the Brokenhearted

Me and My Big Mouth!

Me and My Big Mouth! Study Guide

Prepare to Prosper

Do It Afraid!

Expect a Move of God in Your Life…Suddenly!

Enjoying Where You Are on the Way to Where You Are Going

The Most Important Decision You Will Ever Make

When, God, When?

Why, God, Why?

The Word, the Name, the Blood

Battlefield of the Mind

Battlefield of the Mind Study Guide

Tell Them I Love Them

Peace

The Root of Rejection

If Not for the Grace of God

If Not for the Grace of God Study Guide

JOYCE MEYER SPANISH TITLES

Las Siete Cosas Que Te Roban el Gozo
(Seven Things That Steal Your Joy)

Empezando Tu Día Bien (Starting Your Day Right)

BY DAVE MEYER

Life Lines